AF441185

LOVE IN A PETBOOK

ALISON R. LANIER

Copyright 2021 by Alison Lanier

This book is protected under the copyright laws of the United States of America. Any reproduction or other unauthorized use of the material or artwork herein is prohibited. All rights reserved.

Book Cover Design by Nicole Martini

CONTENTS

*Dedicated to my very first dog,
Marvelous Magnificent Dog (Marvy).
Your name preceded and succeeded you.
You surpassed all my wildest expectations
of unconditional love.*

*What if one day
you never make it home again?
Pets are waiting on you ...
What happens next?*

ACKNOWLEDGMENTS

This book has been a dream in my mind for far too many years. It's truly a blessing to finally get it out.

I'd like to acknowledge my family for their everlasting encouragement, and I'd like to thank all my present and previous pet interactions outside of my immediate household - for without my family and all those pets, I never would have found my courage.

Grey, talk about having my back and coming at me with complete honesty ... a million thank-you's. You got it from the beginning. But you've always gotten me. Thank you. I never could have done this without you.

Sonam, Varun & Cooper the Silver Lab, I'm in awe of all the life spirits that brought you into my life for so many positive reasons; way too many to list here, Thank you all.

Sarah W., your creative talent and direction has taken me to a life level I never envisioned. Thank you. Your organizational skills put my Virgo senses to shame.

Cousin Carolyn, thank you for recognizing the vision early on, typing up all those early notes and compiling it into a neat folder that reminded me not to let my idea die; thank you for your relenting encouragement.

Pet Parent Community, thank you for realizing the possibilities this book holds. Thank you for loving your own pets enough to document the love given throughout their lives.

I am forever grateful to **Jeremy Herman**, who has taken my book to a higher professional level than even I envisioned. You truly have amazing formatting skills. You saw things I never even visualized and you were able to take my book there. Thank you for being a huge part of this creation.

BEGINNINGS AND ENDINGS HAPPEN

More times than not, it is our beloved pets who leave us before we leave them. Some literally go off to die, yet for others, after illness comes about, the decision to euthanize is a gut-wrenching decision to make as a pet parent, but also a necessary loving act to do when your fur baby has expressed to you that they can no longer hang on. Rarely do we, as pet parents, contemplate what happens to our pets if we ourselves just don't make it home.

As a previous pet sitter and dog walker, I witnessed this firsthand. I sat for a pet parent who went on a two-week vacation to another country, was involved in an accident and never returned home. I fostered her two fur babies until her next of kin arrived and fortunately, he was more than willing to take both pets with him.

A second scenario - I was a weekly dogwalker to a newly

acquired puppy of an elderly woman. Unexpectedly this woman fell, was hospitalized and passed away. She dearly loved her puppy but had made no contingency plans for his care. Fortunately, her daughter was able to take the puppy into her home and he is now living an extremely charmed life.

The last scenario I was involved in, unfortunately I have no outcome to report. It involved a pet parent scheduled for heart surgery. Recovery would take a few months and she would not be able to have any interaction with her cat Stella while she recovered. She had no family left and no friends capable of caring for her beloved cat. She petitioned me to assist her in finding a care giver to step in for the two months post-surgery. She was also looking for a new pet parent in the event she didn't survive. I met with her to help her find a suitable caregiver even though I lived one state over from her at the time.

What I took from our meeting was how detail oriented she was about Stella. Reciting to me how she came to adopt Stella only after watching her be adopted out and returned three times prior by others. She vowed not to have anyone else adopt Stella except her because she knew how emotionally challenged Stella had become by all the adoption events. She recited to me how finicky an eater Stella was, resulting from a gum condition, and how you had to "pill" Stella in a certain way, and how she only meowed when en route to the vet's office ... on and on our conversation went. I came to know Stella extremely well through her pet parents' words. I admired the love and overall wellbeing this woman had for her cat.

Unfortunately, even two months prior to surgery, a suitable caregiver had not been found for Stella. My notes regarding a suitable caregiver were passed on to another person as I moved away from the state shortly thereafter.

Fast forward to 2020 when Covid-19 hit the world with a vengeance, and by 2021 we lost millions to this horrendous pandemic. Those who survived this disease often found their world completely changed by loss of loved ones, loss of job, loss of home or all the above. There was even loss of pet(s) that media didn't talk too much about. One such individual found herself fighting random financial hardships; all within a span of five months compounded by Covid – she lost her job and then she lost her house. She was so determined to not lose her 6-month-old German Shepard puppy, she resorted to sleeping in her car. But after realizing this situation wasn't safe for either one of them or even fair for her puppy to go through, she slept on the floors and couches of trusted friends. When this became infringing, her only option was to move in with her mother who lived in an apartment that did not allow pets. Eventually she posted social media pleas, urgently asking for adoptees or foster groups to take in her precious German Shepard. Posting cutesy photos and brief personality traits, I'm sure she vehemently fought through tears as she typed her plea onto Facebook. I can only imagine the gut-wrenching task of handing over the leash and saying goodbye to her trusted pal when an adoptable opportunity was finalized.

I wish this book had been in her possession prior to this happening because it wasn't only her emotions experiencing loss, but her German Shephard experienced it as well. Even at 6 months old, rituals had been established that would have been important in helping transition this puppy into its new home. Imagine if she had been able to hand over her puppy's *Love in a PetBook* along with a blanket or t-shirt of hers to faster acclimate her puppy to its newly acquired pet parent. The transition would have been more self-assuring with a PetBook than without.

So, these are only a few reasons why this book, this *Love in a PetBook* is absolutely necessary for the pets we love who look to us for their continued care. It's needed because a small percentage out of the 6.5 million pets entering animal shelters annually[1] are there because their owners have passed away. Of course, there are other contributing factors to pets ending up in animal shelters that don't involve the death of a pet parent. Some of which include pets getting out of their homes without any identification, pets being surrender, moving, health concerns, money, kids and behavioral issues.

Imagine a book such as this following a surrendered cat or dog into an animal shelter. Imagine the next possible forever family looking through this book to determine if the pet they think they're in love with, will be a perfect match for their home. Knowing what good and bad habits the pet displays, will greatly accelerate the adoption process.

Fortunately, about 3.2 million shelter animals are adopted each year[2]. If you've ever adopted a pet, you already know the process it takes to find forever homes. Think about the resources and the staff it takes to place an adopted pet in your home ... It takes a village. This is a vast operation involving pet loving volunteers, adoption facilities, individual foster homes, transportation, donations and fundraising events to find suitable forever homes for those not able to be returned to their rightful owner. This book honors pets and the people who love them. This is *Love in a PetBook* for every household that considers their pet family.

HOW TO USE THIS BOOK

This book is a guideline resource, an advocate for your pet as only you know them through your experience. This book is not meant to be a legally binding entity. I suggest you see a lawyer and implement a legal will for that. What this book does is assists the next pet caregiver, whomever they may be, to succeed in the loving care and happiness of your beloved pet in all ways possible. Should you be fortunate enough to never have to use this book to bequeath your pet to a caregiver, then I hope this book becomes a joyful remembrance of your pet(s) life well lived.

Whichever way this book is used, take the time to purposely observe your interactions with your pet(s) over a day, a week, a month, and observe your pet(s) activities, likes, dislikes, etc. This book is way beyond your pet(s) food type, food schedule or vet record information, it's their personality shining through the pages telling a potential adoptive family I'm for you or I'm not for you. Honesty is key. You love your pet(s) just the way they are, trust that there's another family out there that will too. Put yourself in the "observers" eyes as if you were handing over the keys to your fortune – because you are. Direct the next caregiver on how to successfully handle your fortune through your words.

So, let's begin:

Initially you will need to select a responsible person as a caregiver for your pet(s). And by 'responsible' I mean, an individual who is clearly aware of how much your pet means to you and is aware of your lifestyle as it revolves around your pet(s). I highly suggest selecting at least two individuals just in case circumstances change in one of their own lives. Clearly communicate to them what your wishes are as being a caregiver to your pet(s). Communicate to them whether you expect them to take your pet(s) into their home as their own, whether you expect them to be the transporter for your pet(s) and all their belongings to another individual in another state or taken to a pet sanctuary designated by you. They will need to have access to your pet(s), to their things, and to this book that you are filling out on their behalf.

Currently, my own personal situation involves having two hairless Chinese Cresteds. They are six years old at the time of this writing. We have a very active lifestyle of hiking, paddle boarding, kayaking and e-biking; I honestly am unable to list any individual caregivers for them. What I have done for my circumstance, however, is to identify a responsible individual who can transport them to a Chinese Crested rescue facility of my choice, along with their book to ensure they are adopted together to a more active family. So, a rescue facility can also serve as caregiver if you have no individual resources available to you as well.

Now, for those of you wondering why an active family would be my choice for my two babies even if they may be well into their senior years should I pass. It's because even a senior dog can get stressed and I know floating on a lake in a kayak will soothe their soul. And even though they might not be up to long hikes anymore, being placed in a doggie back-pack and allowing them to be able to smell the freshness of mountains, woods or grass, would greatly feed their soul.

Things like this you'll need to keep in mind as you fill out this book.

All your words on behalf of your pet will need to be docu-mented by you in the latter portion of this book. The chapter called **References A thru Z** has been alphabetized in such a manner that a new caregiver can quickly look up any topics they might want to know about your baby from A to Z. For example, let's say a new caregiver wants information on giving your pet a bath. They can simply refer to the word 'Bath' to look at any notes you may have included. You, on the other hand may have included all your bathing notes under the word 'Grooming'; so instead of rewriting everything under 'Bath', simply put a notation saying, "see Grooming".

Many words within **Reference A to Z** will have similar meanings; most of these words will have little paw markers next to them ( ). Paw markers will indicate words that can become interchangeable i.e., Veterinarian and Doctor, can all point to the same notation. Just choose the word you most closely identify with and place a notation next to any other similar words, pointing the reader back to your chosen word.

Get creative with your descriptions. Remember, the reader is learning about your pet through your words. If you put peanut butter on your forehead to capture your pet's attention as you clip their nails, write that down, it's important. If you sing to them in the morning, write that down, it's important. The next caregiver may not sing, but it will explain a lot if that song plays on the radio and your pet suddenly goes crazy.

About the other chapters:

Just The Basics For Any Pet Parent – This chapter includes information that should be kept readily available in any pet household. These tips and resources will assist you in preparing for emergencies involving your pet(s). This is not a complete list of things to have, only the basic things to have on hand.

About My beloved Pet – This chapter documents your

pet(s) name, gender, breed, eating schedule, weight, etc. It is just meant to be basic information for a quick lookup.

Say Cheese! Photos Go Here – Pretty self-explanatory, this is a page to include one or two pictures of your pet. Either tape or paste to the page. There is also a line to include the name(s) of any social media page your pet may have. I would include at least one photo that depicts something about your pet that might be difficult to explain in words i.e., a picture of your dog balancing a ball on his nose or your cat riding in a kayak.

In Your Own Words – This chapter is for you to document your love story about your pet. It's subtitled *how I came to meet my pet and what I love about them*. Freestyle anything you have to say about the first time you met your pet, the first time you knew you were a team, or whatever else is amazing about your beloved pet.

Message to a Caregiver – This chapter is for you to tell a potential caregiver thank you, or who you hope they are to your pet, or anything that comes to mind that they should know from your heart.

Quick Pet Reference Dog or Cat – This is a critical chapter for any potential adoptable family to quickly scan your pet abilities and/or behavioral concerns. This Reference section will prove most important should your pet ever end up in a shelter or foster care situation. It's a quick reference compatibility guide that needs to be filled out accurately in order to properly match your pet to their next forever family.

<u>References A Thru Z</u> – This section is where all the attention to detail about your pet comes into play. These pages will contain a lot of necessary documentation that can only be done by you; alphabetized to allow any caregiver easy access to words under the section they're searching for. For example, wondering about any nose issues? Go to '**N**' and lookup nose. If you run out of writing room, each section should have space at the end to continue your notes as well as adding additional words not found in its designated section.

JUST THE BASICS FOR ANY PET PARENT

What a basic pet plan should include:

SELECT at least two responsible friends or relatives to be a temporary emergency caregiver. They should be willing to execute your wishes regarding your pet(s) in the event you aren't around. Provide them with keys, leash location, feeding instructions, name of your veterinarian, location of this PetBook, and general care instructions.

Make sure close friends and/or relatives know how many pets you have and the name and contact numbers of the individuals who have agreed to serve as emergency caregiver. All emergency caregivers should also know how to contact each other as well.

Include emergency contact names and numbers with your veterinarian.

Carry a wallet 'Alert Card' listing the type of pets you have and the name and phone number of your emergency pet caregiver. Alert Card variations can be found online.

Download an 'in case of emergency app' (I.C.E.)

Keep copies of all pertinent pet information in a grab bag conveniently located in your house in case of emergency evacuation such as fire, tornado, etc. You'll need this to bring your pets with you into a temporary evacuation shelter.

Discuss caregiving pet options with your family/friends.

Complete a personal ***Love in a PetBook*** for every pet in the household and make sure family/friends and caregivers know where to access it. Write your pets name along the spine of this book for easy identification.

ABOUT MY BELOVED PET:

Name

____

____

Nicknames

____

____

Cat/Dog__________Age__________ Male/Female___________

Breed/Best Guess

____

____

Weight________

Color/Markings

Eating schedule

Medical conditions

Disabilities

SAY CHEESE! PHOTOS GO HERE

(A few pics for the book – paste here)

ALISON R. LANIER

Identifying markers:

____

____

____

____

Social Media page to refer to:

____

____

____

____

How I came to meet my pet and what I love about them:

____

____

____

____

____

____

____

____

____

____

____

____

MESSAGE TO A CAREGIVER

Add a personalized note to your caregiver:

____

____

____

____

____

____

____

____

____

____

____

____

QUICK REFERENCE DOG

Walks on leash

Yes ..... No

Anxiety Issues

Yes ..... No

Howls/barks/cries when alone

Yes ..... No

Can use doggy door

Yes ..... No

Afraid of thunder

Yes ..... No

Leash aggressive

Yes ..... No

Food aggression

Yes ..... No

Good with kids

Yes ..... No

Good with other dogs

Yes ..... No

Good with cats

Yes ..... No

Crate trained

Yes ..... No

Crated when you're gone

Yes ..... No

Likes car rides

Yes ..... No

Enjoys walks

Yes ..... No

Walks with collar

Yes ..... No

Walks with harness

Yes ..... No

Walks with gentle leader

Yes ..... No

Pees indoors

Yes ..... No

Uses pee pads

Yes ..... No

Uses belly bands

Yes ..... No

Enjoys dog parks

Yes ..... No

Plays ball

Yes ..... No

Knows a few commands

Yes ..... No

Gets on furniture

Yes ..... No

Barks at other dogs

Yes ..... No

Calmly bathed

Yes ..... No

Can open doors/cabinets

Yes ..... No

Bites

Yes ..... No

Likes to be carried

Yes ..... No

Can handle stairs

Yes ..... No

Wears clothes

Yes ..... No

Sleeps on bed

Yes ..... No

QUICK REFERENCE CAT

Needs covered litter box

Yes ..... No

Needs clay kitty litter

Yes ..... No

Prefers wet food

Yes ..... No

Prefers dry food

Yes ..... No

Good with kids

Yes ..... No

Good with other cats

Yes ..... No

Good with other dogs

Yes ..... No

Sprays indoors

Yes ..... No

Opens doors/cabinets

Yes ..... No

Needs to wear a bell

Yes ..... No

Wears collar

Yes ..... No

Wears harness

Yes ..... No

Tolerates baths

Yes ..... No

Plays with toys

Yes ..... No

Uses scratch pads

Yes ..... No

Scratches furniture

Yes ..... No

Fearful of thunder

Yes ..... No

Very playful

Yes ..... No

Sleeps on bed

Yes ..... No

Leash trained

Yes ..... No

Indoor/outdoor cat

Yes ..... No

Likes to be held

Yes ..... No

Likes to be brushed

Yes ..... No

Knows a few commands

Yes ..... No

Uses a doggie door

Yes ..... No

Tolerates crate transport

Yes ..... No

Tolerates car rides

Yes ..... No

Bites

Yes ..... No

Nocturnal play

Yes ..... No

Declawed

Yes ..... No

Strong hunting tendencies

Yes ..... No

Enjoys catnip

Yes ..... No

REFERENCES A THRU Z

A

Abandonment Issues

Affectionate

After Alarm Goes Off

After Eating

After Walking

After Car Rides

Afternoon

Aggression

Agility

Airplane

Allergies

Anal Express

Animal Types *(that pet is used to)*

Anxiety

Apples

Arriving Home

Arthritis

Awards

B

Balloons

Balls

Bananas

Barking

Bathtime

Bed Stairs

Bicycle (*habits with/around one*)

Bites

Belly Rubs

Blanket (*favorite kind/type*)

🐾 Bowls

🐾 Breakfast

Broken Tail

🐾 Brushing

Bubbles

Burial *(wishes for your pet)*

Butt Scooches

C

Cameras (*doggie cam*)

____

____

____

____

____

Cancer

____

____

____

____

____

Caregiver (*designated person*)

Carpet

Car Rides

Car Seat

Carrots

Catnip

Ceiling Fans

Chases

Cheese

Chewer

Claws

Cleaning Products Used

Climbs (*fences/trees*)

Clinic

Close Pet Pals

Closets (*hides/sleeps in*)

Clothes

Cold Days

Collars

Comb

Commands

Cone *(ever had to wear one)*

Coughing

Covers

🐾 Crates

🐾 Cremation (*wishes for your pet after they pass*)

Cries (*cries when...*)

Curiosity (*how curious is your pet*)

D

Daytime Routines

Death (*Quick tips to shorten the mourning period of another pet/person*)

Declawed (*how long*)

🐾 Deliveries to House

🐾 Dental Cleaning

Digging

🐾 Dinner

🐾 Doctor

Doesn't Like

Dog Carriers

Dog Events (*ever attended*)

Dog Food (*type/homemade/amount*)

Dog Park

Dog Seat

Doggy Daycare *(ever been/experience)*

Doors *(can pet open)*

Doorbell

🐾 Down Command

E

Ears

Eating Habits

Erratic Behaviors

Expandable Leash

Eye Boogers

Eye Problems

F

Favorite Toy

Feces (eats own/eats others?)

Feeding (schedule/amount)

Females (afraid of)

Fences (jumps over, needs one, etc.)

Feral

Fetches

Fireworks

Flea Treatment

Flooring (carpet/hardwood/issues)

Flying (has your baby flown?)

Food

Fourth of July

Free Feeder

Flying (has your baby flown?)

Fun

Funeral (would you like your pet to attend yours?)

Furniture (allowed on, chews on, has own)

G

Games We Play

Gas/Gassy (intestinal issues)

Gentle Leader Collar

Grass (eats?)

Greets You at the Door

Greets Other Dogs Well

🐾 Grooming

Groomer Information

H

Hair/Haircut (tolerance/style)

Hair Koss

Halloween (afraid of costumes)

Happiness

🐾 Hardwood Floors

🐾 Harness (wears one)

Hats

Hides

Hiking

Hip Problems

Holidays

Hot Days

Hot Spots

Hours Spent Alone

Housebroken

House Rules

Howling

Humping

Hurricane (hiding spot/routine)

Hydrotherapy

Ice Chips

____

____

____

____

____

____

Ice Cream

____

____

____

____

____

Ignores Or Hides when....

Injuries (past/present)

J

Jowls (skin around mouth)

Jumping

Kayaking

Kennels Inside House

Keys (who has key access)

Kid Friendly

Kisses

Kitchen Rules

Kind to Strangers

L

Lap Time

____

____

____

____

____

____

Leash (type/pulls)

____

____

____

____

____

Leave It Command

Licking

Life Vest

Litter Box

Litter Products

Loud Noises

Lovin on You

Lunch

M

Mailperson / Deliveries

Maintenance People in The House

Massage

Messes/Tears Things

Males (afraid of?)

Medicine

🐾 **Meeting Others** (dogs, visitors)

🐾 **Men** (partial to)

Moods

Mouse catcher

🐾 **Mourning** (how does your pet grieve)

Music

Nails

Natural Disasters (ever been thru one)

Neutered

New Surroundings

Nicknames

No-Nos

Nose (issues)

○

🐾 Opens Doors

____

____

____

____

____

____

Other Types of Animals *(reaction to horses, deer, etc.)*

____

____

____

____

____

Outside

Overnight Guest

P

Paddleboards

Peanut Butter

Pee Pads

Peeing Habits

Personal Songs

Personality

🐾 **Pictures** (*with Santa/Easter Bunny*)

🐾 **Pills**

Pill Pockets

Plant Eater

Play Pal

Playing / Playfulness

Poop (*usual consistency/eats*)

Popcorn

🐾 Pulls

Purrs

🐾 Purse (*Pocket Pooch*)

Puzzles

Q

Quakes

____

____

____

____

____

____

Quiet

____

____

____

____

____

Quinoa

R

Radio (*do you leave on when gone*)

Rain

Raincoat

Rash (*what causes rashes*)

Recall (*comes when called*)

Rubs Against You

S

Safe Spaces

Santa *(pictures/afraid of)*

Scratching

Scratch pad

Scooches (*butt across floor*)

Seizures

Shampoo (*type used*)

Sheds (*a little or a lot*)

Shoes (*wears / eats them*)

Shots

Sick (*how you can tell*)

Singing (*to your pet/pet sings to you*)

Sitters (*ever have one*)

Skateboards (*knows how/runs next to*)

Sleep Habits

Snores

Snow (*experience with*)

Soap

Sounds

Spayed

Sprays

Stairs

🐾 Stay

Stores (*how do they act inside*)

Storms

Stubborn about ...

Sulking

Sunscreen

Swimming

T

T-Shirts (*favorite shirt*)

____

____

____

____

____

____

Table Food

____

____

____

____

____

Tail

Tease Play

Teeth

Television (*TV – leave on?*)

Therapy Pet (*Officially registered as*)

Thunder

Toothpaste

Tornado (*hide spot/routine*)

Toys *(types / favorite)*

Train Rides

🐾 Travel

Treadmill

Tricks

Trashcan (*need a special one / digger?*)

U

Under Foot (*in between your feet*)

Urinates in the House

Usual Routine

V

Vacations

Vaccinations

Vacuum Cleaner

Veterinarian Office

Visitors

Vocal *(when pet is most vocal)*

Voice Commands

W

Walking (*likes / duration / how often*)

Water

Weather

Website (*does your pet have one*)

Wheelchair (*use of wheels to get around*)

Window Barking

Wipes (*to clean feet*)

Women (*partial to*)

$$X$$

X Marks The Spot (*favorite spots to walk/visit/carried*)

X Rays (*ever had one*)

Y

Yardwork (*afraid of lawnmowers/rakes*)

Yelling (*pets' reaction to it*)

Yogurt

Yuckiness

Yours / Not Yours (see commands)

Yummies (what's yummy to your pet)

Z

Zombies (ok, this was put in just for fun, but is your pet
afraid of zombie house play or costumes?)

____

____

____

____

____

Zoomies

____

____

____

____

____

AFTERWORD

It's never the end of a life, even when the book closes. I commend you for completing your ***Love in a PetBook*** on behalf of your precious pet(s); now go hug and kiss em hard, because you've now earned a sense of peace among uncertainty.

NOTES

Beginnings and Endings Happen

1. Data compiled 2015-2018 Shelter Animals Count & American Pet Products Association (APPA)
2. Data compiled 2015-2018 Shelter Animals Count & American Pet Products Association (APPA)

2015 was the year I lost my Aunt Clara. I loved her very much as we shared many great times. Several years prior to her illness, I even gifted her a papillon puppy she named Ruby. Ruby and Aunt Clara were inseparable, especially after my uncle passed away and Aunt Clara became widowed. I'm sure it was Ruby that helped Aunt Clara the most to get through those tough times of loss after all the other relatives went on about their lives.

During Aunt Clara's illness and ultimately her death, the question remained, "who would care for Ruby?" Aunt Clara's kids all lived out of state, her granddaughter was local but had a family of her own with special needs kids to care for. I, of course, wanted Ruby, but at that time, with 6 dogs of my own, I wasn't sure how a one-person dog would transition to such a busy household.

In the end however, everything worked out well for Ruby. She lives happily with Aunt Clara's daughter accompanying her to work and even vacationing together.

So, it was after my experience with Aunt Clara and Ruby

that I asked myself, who would care for my own dogs in the event of an unexpected disability, illness or death? I couldn't name one person to handle all 6 of my dogs, but I knew if I could pair off a few; provide each with their own manual or guidebook, they would have a better chance of being well cared for in the short term and stand a better chance of being adopted in the long term should the situation arise. I knew which of my babies would stress the most and I knew what a care giver could do to greatly reduce that stress. A momma knows, a pet parent just knows; so, I created this book to bridge the wishes of pet parent to caregiver. To strengthen and quicken any pet's ability to find their next forever home, perhaps reducing or even eliminating animal shelter stays.

Ever since I began paying my own way in life, whether in an apartment or a house, I've always had cats and/or dogs. They've soothed my soul always and helped keep me active. They've comforted me through tough days and served as the best litmus test for boyfriends, girlfriends and roommates. I can't imagine my life without a pet in it.

As a shy, much younger lady, socializing was awkward for me. Conversation icebreakers were always more interesting if asked about pets. So, it was no surprised when my life shifted to pet sitting, or delighting in finding homes for strays, instead of hanging out with the crowd. I created businesses around pets for many years involving making clothes, hats, carrier bags, pet walking, pet sitting and even hosted a charity pet fashion show. Today however, my main focus is on what I can do to help more pets find lasting, compatible homes. *Love In A PetBook* is here to help with that. No matter what, pets and the people who love them will always remain dear to my heart.

www.ingramcontent.com/pod-product-compliance
Lightning Source LLC
Chambersburg PA
CBHW061259120726
48001CB00001B/381